The Pearl of Night

Rachel Lawson

The Pearl of Night

Poetry, Volume 1

Rachel Lawson

Published by Rachel Lawson, 2022.

Table of Contents

The Pearl of Night

The sky is a diamonds upon onyx,
floating in the sky is the pearl of night,
it drifts in like a bright shining pearl,
rolling around the sky with an elegant heart stealing charm,
enchanting the soul with it's pure beauty

The Rose

What is a rose the heart's en-trapper,
The senses captor,
Lover to the eye,
The nose's soul mate,
With a touch of pain with it's thorn

Red Sails in the Sunset

Sailing with the sunset,
three silhouettes of yachts sail on a grey dappled river,
the sun a white orb above the land in the horizon,
the sky is aflame,
grey, red tinged clouds sail by in the skies above,
below sails a yacht with sails glowing red in the sunset's light.

Wispy white cotton candy clouds v2

Wispy white cotton candy clouds sail upon a sky of zenith blue,

flying over fields of green,

the clouds turn grey and water the fields below,

they skip above oceans, rivers, and seas, in the breeze,

float over cities and towns,

like waves, they blow over deserts dry,

raining down on forests and tropics hard,

planes above and through them fly,

clouds feed tree and grass with rain,

rain freezes into snow and coarse frozen hail,

types of clouds are,

fluffy non-rain clouds,

clouds like paintings,

grayish tinged rain clouds,

some look like waves in the sea

Walking on the Stars

I am walking on the milky way,
I am walking through space,
I take a stride between Earth and Mars,
Ride the solar wind between here and there,
where can I go there almost anywhere,
I do so without care

Snow Blossom

Delicate sweetly scented snow falls from the cherry tree,
in springs bower it rains upon the ground,
the snow steals the heart and soul with its beauty and airs,
it is a special snow it releases an aura of perfume
the tree flowers for a short time but it is a lovely time the time of its flowers

On the Wings of the Wind

On the wings of the wind
riding the wind like leaf in the air,
swift as an eagle on the wing,
flies the swallow on the wing,
through the air like an acrobat she flies,
small and delicate,
sweet and swift,
it is a little angel on the wing

The Sweeter the Rose to Me

A rose is a beauty with a smell divine.
it steals my heart and soul,
with its beauty and scent.
I wish I could see it I have no eyes,
sadly I can't smell it I have no nose,
but at least the thorns can't hurt my hand,
mused a grim reaper holding a lovely red rose

Shadow of the Moon

the moon is dark,
the moon is new,
the stars are bright,
they are the only things in the sky,
they are like silver diamond twinkling in the darkness,
they are little suns far away,
enchanting the mind and soul with their sweet sparkly twinkle

The Clouds of Dreams

Clouds float through the skies of blue like ethereal sprites,
hoping over green fields far below,
clouds cry on the grass,
skip like stones over oceans river and seas, in the breeze,
flowing over cities and town like rivers in the sky,
flow like waves on the shore over deserts dry,
falling down refreshing forests and tropics,
clouds are hard to predict and know,
the rain feeds many a tree and the grass with its water,
in the cold hearts of clouds freeze into rain and hail,
clouds come in many types and forms,
grey tempest storms,
light fluffy clouds which bring no rain,
water color like clouds like dreams,
the greyish rain bearers,
some resemble sea wave in the sky,
they are the bringers of dreams people see dreams in them,
these dreams are false,
others claim to predict their ways,
and some are wrong,
clouds are ethereal things.

Escaping from my mind

I am stuck in my mind lost in my thoughts,
unable to escape a prison of my own design,
the prison of my conciousness,
I want to leave my prison and live in the world outside,
why must I be entrapped by my inner world?
how can I escape a world I cannot see?
lost in my own fears,
lost in my own realm of internal hell,
never to escape,
never to be free

Stars

Ancient fires of antiquity,
burning lights in the dark of night,
illuminating the soul of night,
sentinels from the part long gone,
not all are there still where they are seen now,
some are have burnt their last millennia ago,
they are ghosts of the past seen in a future how long ago from them and us it is beyond our comprehension.

The Welcome Swallow

Where do you go,
oh sweet little bird,
pretty pilot of the skies,
please come again,
you are always very welcome,
my dear friend the welcome swallow.

My Pet Human

I am just an average goldfish,
I have a job like everyone else,
I wind down watching my favorite pet human,
I watch him walking around his tank,
I watch him talking to my other pet humans in the tank,
I wonder what he's saying to them,
I find it quite relaxing after a busy day at work.

Under The Golden Moon extended

The cloud smothered sky has a golden glow betraying the wildfire to come, the trees are shadows waiting to burn. The tire tracks of the road glows like trails of fire burning in two rows.

Softly Falls The Rain

Softly falls the rain, through the air cool, clear and crisp,
from the skies above, slowly falling to the ground,
falls the nectar of the sky, the balm of the Earth,
that moisturises soil, and nourishes the plants,
it the fills the oceans with it's waters, for the fish in it to swim,
and upon it men to sail, to catch the fish and
after the water brings life to the world. it returns to it's sky home and
waits to fall again.

What's Left Unsaid

The biggest regret is not unfinished thoughts,
It is what is unsaid the goodbyes, the I love yous and the like,
the things undone, the last thoughts of people would
seldom be on thoughts unthought because they rarely come to mind,
at least as import actions or lack of actions cause more pain.

Trial By Stone

He who pulls the sword from the stone is the once and future king.
He who pulls the sword from the stone about people will sing,
He who pulls the sword from the stone is cursed,
He who pulls the sword from the stone will be betrayed,
He who pulls the sword from the stone will die,
He who pulls the sword from the stone will in Avalon Lie.

The Sparkling Skies Above

The stars are beautiful sparkling diamonds up on a dark velvet sky,
they twinkle in constant rhythm in the cool refreshing night's air
enchanting the heart and the soul down to the core

Lady of the Lake

Lady of the Lake she was called,
she was a nymph enchantress from beneath the waves,
she was the guardian of the sword Excalibur,
she gave King Arthur it and was on his death returned to her,
she lived in a castle below the water of a lake near Avalon,
she raised his betrayer Lancelot when his father died,
hence his name Lancelot of the Lake,
she was killed by another knight called Sir Balin,
over a deadly feud of divergence,
he blamed her for his mother's death,
she blamed him over her brother's death,
the knight beheaded her in Avalon,
so fell the the fair nymph,
known as Nimue the Lady of the Lake.

While the World was Sleeping

I lived my life while the world was sleeping,
I took my first breath when the world was laughing,
I took my first step when the world was crying,
I took my last breath when the world wasn't looking.

The Dream

To live for the moment and to die for memories of those moments lived, but not dreams which never came to be. That is what should be.

The Marvellous Light

Crystalline pure silvery aura of night,
is within my sight,
the moon glows full and bright,
it is a marvellous light.

Riding the waves of time

I ride the waves of time,
I live in the past, present, and future for a while,
I know what has come to be,
I know not what will come to be,
I know the past like an old friend,
I ride through the present upon the wake of the past to the future,
I was born in the past and will die in the future one grave day

Breaking through the wall

Going beyond hitting the wall,
Is hard not too not only for me but all,
It's like banging your head into a brick wall,
Your stamina and strength are lost none left to recall,
You cannot go on you are left fearing you may fall,
You need the cool chilling healing balm of rest for it to stall,
But you must go on beyond the wall,
You cannot stop until you breach that wall.

The Unicorn

Equine beauty,
pure and elegant in its innocence,
a fantastic beast,
wild stallion of myth,
a timeless creature of another world,
rare horse of a horse of dreams,
lost in the minds of man.

Like a Moth to a Flame

Humans chase the sun like a moth to a flame,
we rise with the sun and hibernate when the sun leaves,
We adore her sister the moon who is lit by the sun's loving glow,
The sun warms our hearts in our Earthly bower.

When We Were Young

When we were young the world was magical,
When we were young we were immortal,
When we were young the world was ours,
When we were young we could do anything,
When we were young our dream would all come true,
When we were young nothing could stop us,
When we were young love would find us,
When we were young anything was possible,
When we were young the world was a dream,
When we were young the world was our pearl,
When we were young fantasy was real,
When we were young we were all swashbuckling heroes,
When we were young no one could stop us,
When we were young we were dreamers,
When we were young romance was real,
When we were young there was always a happy ending.

In My Life

I have lived a life in dreams,
not all is as it seems,
everything is running as theme,
it's a lovely dream,
melting into a pool of happiness and pain,
like a bitter-sweet refrain,
sang by a melancholy singer in a song so sweet,
I know the future I will meet,
with similar heartfelt empathy as I do the past,
all comes and goes until days last.

A thousand million eyes

They say the night has a thousand eyes,

That "One could not count the moons that shimmer on her roofs, or the thousand splendid suns that hide behind her wall."

Beautiful sparkling eyes of stars the lonely travellers of the skies,

thy light charms all,

thy fires eternally burn,

the silvery beams from moons and suns illuminate the night with night's alluring glow

the light of these hundred million suns and moons illuminate lovers perpetual yearn,

they are distant and far memories of days aeons ago.

A Moon Shadow Nocturne

A play of light and dark,
under the wan light of the moon plays with the skipping shadows of
night's dance their bewitching saraband with the moonlight,
silver moonlight and darkness melt into one in the cool airs of the
nocturnal bower of night,
the stars sparkle in the shadows far above the worldly cradle of man,
it is pure enchantment by moonlight,
a nocturne of moonlight and shadows melding it to one,
a song both dark and light with an ethereal heady air of enchantment
leaving the heart aglow

The Eyes of Night

They say the night has a thousand eyes,
not many know the hows or whys,
they are the stars of light,
they are a beautiful sight,
they are the burning embers of stars long past,
they are the eyes of the night to their last,
when they close their eyes in fire or ice,
till their ends, someone always says it nice,

By Candlelight

I read lonely by dim candlelight,

late it is at the night,

the room is scarcely encompassed by the candle's wan glow,

I dream of the new miracle light electric bulb it would Illuminate the darkness as I know,

I curse the dull light of the candle as I can't see to read with it,

with a light bulb, the night's dark aura will submit,

to become like the light of midday,

not the of night pale and dark but with a bulb night's blindness is kept at bay.

Requiem

Under the moon's silver glow,
I could forget everything and live in this moment forever,
tugs on the heartstrings like a beautiful voice in song,
words are the dreams the heart makes,
all now of the dream I have is a requiem.

When The Mirror Cracked

Due to circumstances beyond my control,
the mirror cracked when the bell did toll,
with that, all went wrong,
everything went in flames lifelong,
it felt like ice flowing through my veins,
all I did was in vain me it pains,
it was like fishing without bait,
I tried fixing the mirror but it was too late,
bad luck was all I caught,
I never reached what I sought,
my horse broke its legs,
I dropped a basket of eggs,
milk I spilled,
my dream remains unfulfilled,
misery I feel,
I feel I am trying to hold a slippery eel,
the sharks ate my fish,
I am squeamish,
nothing is going right,
hope is out of sight.

Requiem For a Dream 2

I lament awaking from my dream sublime,
but all sleepers will wake in time,
I feel lost and alone without my dream,
I feel I am missing a vital seam,
I am like a tree broken at the stem,
all now of the dream I have is a requiem.

The Wind Chime

Ting, tink, ting
ting, tink, ting,
the little chimes do sing,
the breeze trough it gently blows,
how long they will ring who knows,
when the wind goes

Haiku By Coup

The haiku form makes no sense to me,
There be neither rhyme nor reason in a haiku to be,
Haiku are maths cross poetry they only confuse,
Mathes and poetry don't well mix that is why to do haiku I refuse.

Breath is life

Life with out breath is death,
I will breathe till my day of my death,
breath is the life of a man,
no breath his death.

Death's Token

Upon my grave do not grieve,
Just leave upon it death's token in reprieve,
A single lily fear not my grave be not chilly,
It is the home of love I am now in heaven far above.

New Ways To Dream

I dream and see any thing can be,
It is a new way to dream for me,
I dream I can do anything,
I am so happy I feel like I can sing,
I could dance I feel high,
People ask me why?
I know my dream to them impossible does seem,
But I have found new ways to dream.

Moonlight on the Water

A sparkling river cool and clear,
enchanted by nature's beauty divine,
pure elegance to the eye and mind.

In The Moonlight Hour

Stillness,
silence,
a cool air,
a silvery glow all around,
pure beauty,
darkness cut by moonlight and starlight.

Thoughts

Life and death all come and go slow and fast,
sad and happy they are,
things come and go,
where will I go? When will I come?

The Night Is Like A Beautiful Gem

The stars are silver sparkling gems floating in the onyx sea of pitch,
the moon like an illuminated glowing gem moonstone that swims
through the starlit sky,
the air is cool and misty upon the lake tonight,
the ground sparkles with its frosty carpet,
the night is like a beautiful gem tonight.

Dreaming

A fantasy world is dreaming,
beyond wakeful deeming,
nothing is as it should be,
nothing is beyond what you can see,
floating through the air,
without a worry or care,
that is all in a dream,
nothing is what it may seem.

The Blue Rose of Egypt

The blue lotus of the Nile,
it is a beauty there is no denial,
drug of the ancients,
its flower bloom requires patience,
it blooms but one time only,
the rose of Egypt bloom is lonely.

Under the dust of the past lie, the days gone by

Under the dust of the past lie, the days gone by
lost in the shadows of time is where the dreams of the past do die,
from the night comes the new days to come,
it is from the dust the grows the world as it will become.

The Dark Side of the Hourglass

The sands in the hourglass creep by briskly,
with the sands fall lives and times and eras,
swift death comes when the sands of life's glass flow of sand stops,
it brings ends to lives, times and all thing within their sands stream
draw to it's end.

The Eternal Flame

I burn with hope like an eternal flame,
the flame ignites a burning bright light,
I see things that never have been seen before,
the fire crackles and illuminates the mind,
the light awakens the soul to new things.

The Sea Horse

Beauty of the sea,
both horse and fish,
hippo-campus, Horse of the seas,
swims and shimmers like a fish,
Poseidon's chariot steed.

Requiem for a Dream v1

I grieve the loss of a dream,
I feel like from me tore a seam,
I lost my faith and hope with it,
I am lost sad and lonely I admit,
I fear life without the dream I bore,
I was happy in the light of my dream before,
I feel my dream has died,
I feel it to me had lied.
will you my dream just fade away,
disappear in an echo of pain one day as dreams do decay.

The Reign of Rain

Cool and softly falls the rain,
from the silvery sky,
it comes sweetly hissing on my roof,
refreshing the world with its life-giving nectar.

Saturn

Rings and diamonds,
a precious gem of space,
planet of ice and rock,
pressure under beauty,
diamonds melting into crystalline liquid diamonds in death.

Ghost Light

By ghost light, the lonely stage is lit,
no one is there it is lit for ghosts alone,
all of the actors are hiding from the stage,
people in crowds are shunned,
the era is one of fear,
so no one even there comes near,
only the ghost of productions past are there.

Time Travel

I am a time traveller, as are we all, we travel through time moment by moment, the possibility of time and chance are considered possible in parallel universes, we all live on in this universal life, balancing upon the tightrope which is time and choice, controlling in which parallel world within which we live and die.

The Rain Falls

I watch as the rain falls,
I here as it calls,
on my tin roof, it hisses,
in calming whispers.
it washes the heat from the air,
the summer heat cools to a temperature easier to bear.

Let it snow

Softly falls the snow,
making hearts aglow,
cool crisp,
floating in a wisp.

Wild flowers

Common some call them,
I am charmed by their wild exotic beauty,
they are to me dear to my heart,
they are elegant delicate beauties of nature,
although some call them weed,
but one man's weed is another's flower,
a dog rose is still a rose,
a wild bluebell still a beauty,
an onion weed still is sweet to the eye,
a flower is still a flower no-matter what you call it.

Mittens Get Off The Television!

Mittens was a cute cat,

on the tv, she sat,

to get my attention,

It was cute but annoying to see her sitting on the television,

I picked her up and told her off,

she was never put off,

she loved attention

she got it did I mention.

The Rose of Snow

Once existed a pure white rose,
from the snow, it rose,
a rose of purest snow,
from the snow, it did grow,
and by the snow, it did die,
in death, it was petals in the snow it did lie.

O, Woe is me

O, Woe is me I am but fate's toy,

I am without joy,

I am a merely fates pawn I maltreated and expendable,

my doom is the only thing I know is the only thing dependable,

I live but for a whim of fate,

I am resigned to my state.

Fiction is the truth inside the lie

One era would say something is true,
another will say it's science fiction or magic or a dream,
in times before it would seem impossible

Two versions of one poem to follow

Not sure the better one so added both

Dick Turpin and the King of the Road

Upon the road, the King, Tom, met Turpin,

Turpin thought King was a fat pigeon,

they rode together on their way,

the robbed people with their guns under the code of the men of the highway,

"The money or your life?" they did call,

it was nothing or all,

Tom made Turpin a highwayman legend,

it was rumoured Turpin brought King's end,

Tom was shot in the shoulder,

he was taken to the Doctor,

he could not be saved,

Turpin, goodbye to the road he waved,

a butcher he became,

he was caught under a charge of poaching claim,

he wrote a letter for help from one of his in-laws,

the only problem was the letter his death's cause,

an old teacher of Turpin's read through his identity fraud,

they knew his handwriting he told truth and not no one could save him not even the good Lord.

he was revealed and caught,

the gallows called according to the court.

death came swiftly,

the legend grew greater hereby.

The King of the Road

Upon the road, Dick Turpin met Tom, the King of the road,
he took Gentleman Tom as a fat pigeon,
as highwaymen in Epping Forest they rode,
Tom taught the code of the highway to Turpin,
it was Tom King who made Dick Turpin a legend,
"Your money or your life" they told anyone unlucky enough to be their beholder,
Turpin it is rumoured was Tom King's end,
Tom was shot through the shoulder,
and was taken to see a surgeon,
they could not save him,
the guilt of killing Tom, was Turpin's burden,
Turpin's end was more strange and grim,
Dick gave up the road,
and became a butcher,
still, at night, he rode,
and was caught as a poacher,
Turpin wrote to his brother-in-law to get him out of jail,
at the jail, his old schoolmaster who had taught him saw the letter, in an act like treason,
Turpin's teacher conspired a betrayal,
it wasn't Turpin's lucky season,
the teacher named the letter's writer,
Turpin was caught,
now he could not get help from his in-law brother,
for his crimes he ended his days at the end of a gallows knot

The End

Don't miss out!

Visit the website below and you can sign up to receive emails whenever Rachel Lawson publishes a new book. There's no charge and no obligation.

https://books2read.com/r/B-A-HMGO-AQHZB

BOOKS2READ

Connecting independent readers to independent writers.

Did you love *The Pearl of Night*? Then you should read *A Moon Shadow Nocturne*[1] by Rachel Lawson!

In author's words on her writing style from her poem The Flow of Magical Words.

"I love words, which pour easily from my pen,

when I put pen to paper a world of words does open,

it flows on the page it's soul mate,

though no one can read the scrawl of words which well inside and opens a gate,

out comes beauty, rhymes of passion, sage words and gloom,

rhyming poem, deathly prose dark as the hand of doom,

the right word is magic in my hand,

like a lover sigh lightly fanned."

---

1. https://books2read.com/u/mB2D1Z

2. https://books2read.com/u/mB2D1Z

Read more at https://rachellawsonpoet.yolasite.com/.

Also by Rachel Lawson

Poetry
Night Poetry
Requiem for a Dream
A Moon Shadow Nocturne
The Pearl of Night
Tempus Fugit Time Flies: Time pieces

Stand and Deliver
In The Moonlight

The Magicians
Getting Good Ratings Is Murder
Blind Faith
Once In a Blue Midnight
The Manchurian Candidate
The Gift And Other Short Stories
The scariest monsters are the ones that lurk within our souls
The Rose
The Mask Magician and other stories
The Man Who Sold The World

Standalone
What The-?

Watch for more at https://rachellawsonpoet.yolasite.com/.

About the Author

Rachel is a lover of gothic poetry and the stories of Emily Dickinsen, Poe, and other poets and writers. she writes in a gothic sometimes romantic, and somewhat eclectic style.

Read more at https://rachellawsonpoet.yolasite.com/.